BBC Children's Books
Published by the Penguin Group
Penguin Books Ltd, 80 Strand, London, WC2R 0RL, England
Penguin Books Australia Ltd, 707 Collins Street,
Melbourne, Victoria 3008, Australia
Canada, India, New Zealand, South Africa

Published by BBC Children's Books, 2012
Text and design © Children's Character Books, 2012

003

Written by Sam Philip

Picture credits: Shutterstock, Karel Gallas, Max Earey, Maksim Toome, Fedor
Selivanov, foto76, loraks, Jerry Horbert, c.byatt-norman, KENCKOphotography,
Christoff, Eve Wheeler Photography, Gustavo Fadel, cjmac, Philip Lange, Patrick
Poendl, Zoran Karapancev, Paulo Manuel Furtado Pires, Tom Wang, Cindy
Haggerty, David Huntley, Andrejs Zavadskis, Pichugin Dmitry, Paul Matthew
Photography, Dudarev Mikhail, Carlos Caetano, Nastenok, Darren Brode,
Dongliu, Richard Fitzer, krutenyukoxana, Shamleen, Paul Stringer, auremar,
meunierd, chert28, Darryl Sleath, Tengku Mohd Yusof bin Tg. Su, Brad Sauter,
Jordan Tan, Marek Gahura, CreativeHQ, cla78, aGinger, AMC Photography,
pio3, steamroller_blues, Ivica Drusany, Dikiiy, Angelo Giampiccolo, WICHAN
KONGCHAN

ISBN: 9781405908467

Printed in China

TopGear
A SPOTTER'S GUIDE

A LITTLE BOOK OF **CARS AND STUFF TO SPOT ON THE ROAD**

INTRODUCTION

Unless you're in the passenger seat of a Bugatti Veyron blasting down a German motorway at 200mph, long car journeys can get a bit boring. Once you've demolished all the food and drink on board, asked 'Are we there yet?' at least 100 times and discovered exactly how angry the driver gets if you quietly remove all the screws from the passenger seat (clue: VERY), there's not much left to do, is there?

Well now there is. The *Top Gear* Spotter's Guide will brighten up even the dullest motorway journey as you hunt out the supercars, weird vehicles, daft road signs, and assorted motoring extras contained within these shiny pages.

THE RULES

The rules are very simple: each of the items contained in this book will earn you points if you spot them out on the road. Some are worth just a single point, some are worth many, but they'll all count towards your score at the end of the journey. Can you set a new personal best?

SOMETHING EXTRA

For real spotting experts, we've included a sneaky extra game. Throughout the book, you'll notice a few of the spots tagged with a symbol. These sneaky specimens activate our cunning two-player game. Here's how it works: first, convince someone else in the car to play against you (if you want to win, it's a good idea to challenge someone with either very poor eyesight or a very bad view of the road). Then get spotting – the first one to spy one of the items in this book and shout it out gets the points: there's no prize for being second! Tot up your points as you go along... but if you spot one of the items marked with this symbol ⚠ first, you can deduct that number of points from your opponent's score!

Best of luck spotting, and remember: you'll need quick eyes to score big points...

EXCELLENT BRITISH STUFF

Britain might not build as many cars as Japan, Germany or the USA, but those that we do are always jolly interesting. Here are some of the finest creations from the greatest country on Earth – give them your stoutest British salute!

CATERHAM

Ever since the company was established in the 1970s, all Caterhams have been based around the same basic platform: Lotus's old 'Seven', a no-frills, rear-wheel drive sports car. But this doesn't mean Caterhams are old and boring: the hottest versions – including the insane R500 – are among the wildest cars in the world!

HOW TO SPOT ONE

BUG-EYED LIGHTS
Stick out on stalks like a shocked chameleon!

NO ROOF
Some Caterhams have a flimsy bit of cloth to protect against the rain, but most are proudly roof-free!

ANY CATERHAM

10 POINTS

TINY STEERING WHEEL
There's not much space in a Caterham's cockpit, not even for a full-size wheel!

ASTON MARTIN

They're probably the most beautiful cars on the planet, and so cool that even James Bond drives one! Some people complain that all Astons look the same... but when they're as pretty as this, is that really a bad thing?

HOW TO SPOT ONE

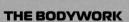

THE BADGE
Check the boot lid for one of these!

THE BODYWORK
If you're thinking, 'Urgh, that's a bit ugly', then you're not looking at an Aston. Everything this company makes is STUNNING.

BIG BONNET
All Astons are front-engined, with either a V8 or V12 churning out lots of power and noise!

A FEW YOU MIGHT SEE

DBS
Roaring V12 supercar, as driven – and crashed – by James Bond in *Casino Royale*.

V8 VANTAGE

A sleek two-seater with a brawny V8 engine, the V8 Vantage is the most popular Aston Martin on the road. Comes in coupé and convertible flavours.

ONE-77

It costs over a million pounds. It has a 7.0-litre V12 engine. It'll remain one of the rarest sights on the road: just seventy-seven were built, of which just a couple remain in Britain. Pity.

ANY ASTON MARTIN   **10** POINTS

ROLLS-ROYCE

The very best of British luxury. Since 1906, Rolls-Royce has been making cars as huge, opulent and expensive as Buckingham Palace's grandest dining rooms – though thankfully they move a bit quicker!

SOME YOU MIGHT SEE

DROPHEAD COUPÉ

What a convertible looks like... if you have enough money to buy Belgium.

20 POINTS — **ANY ROLLS-ROYCE**

HOW TO SPOT ONE

HOOD ORNAMENT
The figure found on every Rolls-Royce bonnet is called 'The Spirit Of Ecstasy'.

UPRIGHT GRILLE
Rolls –Royces are famous for their big, spangly grilles, which are tall and shiny with vertical slats.

ENORMOUS
Rolls-Royces dwarf everything else on the road. The modern Phantom measures nearly six metres in length!

Old, elegant, unruffled – just the sort of car that James May would own. In fact, James May DOES own this car!

PHANTOM
The biggest, poshest and most expensive Rolls. Costs over quarter of a million pounds, weighs nearly three tonnes!

LOTUS

Back in the 1960s, Lotus founder Colin Chapman coined the company's motto: simplify, then add lightness. And Lotus is still doing it today: making super-light, super-agile sports cars that are big on entertainment but short on luxury!

HOW TO SPOT ONE

RACING GREEN
Britain's traditional race shade is the most popular colour for Lotuses. Also watch out for blue, yellow and orange.

SNAKE EYES
Modern Lotuses have drawn-back headlights and gaping mouths. Not pretty, but effective.

AGILE
Lotuses are generally a few hundred kilos lighter than their competitors, so expect to see them darting around the road like dragonflies!

A FEW YOU MIGHT SPOT

ELISE
The most popular and cheapest Lotus. Weighs approximately the same as a bag of flour.

EXIGE
A harder, scarier Elise with a fixed roof and a big wing.

EVORA
Lotus's answer to the Porsche 911. Has a couple of seats in the back, but you wouldn't want to sit there for any longer than a couple of miles!

ANY LOTUS

10
POINTS

DON'T CONFUSE IT WITH...

TESLA ROADSTER
The all-electric sports car is based on a Lotus Elise, but built in California by an American firm.

BENTLEY

The footballers' favourite! Back in the 1920s, Bentley made huge, fast racers that dominated the 24 Hours of Le Mans. Nowadays it builds huge, luxurious, wafty cars favoured by Premier League stars.

SOME YOU MIGHT SEE

1920s BLOWER
After the First World War, this was one of the fastest cars in the world. You're unlikely to see one on the road now though!

BROOKLANDS
The huge coupé that devoured its own tyres during a track test by Jeremy!

ANY BENTLEY

5 POINTS

HOW TO SPOT ONE

BIG ROUND HEADLIGHTS
A design signature. All modern Bentleys feature a double-set of circular 'eyes'.

ENORMOUS
Even the smallest Bentley – the Conti GT – makes 7-Series and S-Classes look petite.

FLASHY GRILLE
Bentley 'mouths' are big and full of chrome. And look very expensive.

CONTINENTAL GT
The sportiest Bentley, and Wayne Rooney's favourite car. Comes in coupé and convertible flavours.

MORGAN

Morgan cars might look like they hail from the 1950s, but under their old-fashioned skins, these machines are surprisingly modern. Richard Hammond owns a Morgan and loves it... but then again he's a bit odd.

HOW TO SPOT ONE

THE BADGE
Wings and a cross, it's as traditional as Morgan itself!

OLD-FASHIONED
Morgan's design book hasn't been updated in a few decades – just look at those 'running boards' that stretch back from the front arches.

MUTED TONES
It simply wouldn't do to have a Morgan in luminous yellow or bright red. Dark greens, blues and silvers are more common.

NO DIGITAL STUFF
In-car television screens? DAB digital radio? Sat nav? Not a chance with the Morgan: things are as traditional and low-tech in here as James May's toolshed.

ANY MORGAN

15 POINTS

SOME YOU MIGHT SPOT

AERO 8

Yes, it has cross-eyes, but the Aero 8 is deceptively fast. Under that traditional bonnet is a brand-new BMW V8 producing over 350bhp!

3-WHEELER

Honestly, this is a brand-new car, not a throwback from the 1930s! When Hammond tested the 3-Wheeler on *Top Gear* TV in 2011, he adored it...

LAND ROVER DEFENDER

It's slower than a combine harvester, it sounds like a tractor and it looks like a filing cabinet on wheels. But, despite all that, the Defender is a true British legend. In production since 1948, the original Land Rover has barely changed over the years...

HOW TO SPOT ONE

BIG AND SQUARE
The Defender doesn't bother with curves or creases. It's flat, it's blocky and you don't mess with it.

ROUND HEADLIGHTS, SQUARE GRILLE
The Defender's traditional face hasn't changed in decades!

FIT FOR PURPOSE
The Defender is available with a hard roof, a soft roof... or even a solid metal boot perfect for transporting sheep!

LAND ROVER DEFENDER

5 POINTS

20

RANGE ROVER EVOQUE

It might look like a full-sized Range Rover, but the Evoque is deceptively tiny: in fact, it's barely longer than a Ford Focus. Victoria Beckham – yes, Posh Spice – had a hand in its design, but don't let that put you off: this is one of the coolest British cars in years!

22

LAND ROVER EVOQUE

4 POINTS

HOW TO SPOT ONE

WEDGY PROFILE
Window-line gets narrower as it reaches the car's tail, giving the Evoque a 'squashed', concept car look.

'FLOATING' ROOF
With its pillars painted dark, the Evoque's roof looks as if it's hovering above the car.

A SPICE GIRL
If you spot a small SUV being driven by a former member of a world-famous girl band – especially one married to a former England footballer – then it's probably the Evoque!

ARIEL ATOM

The coolest thing ever to come out of a West Country shed. Built in Somerset, the flyweight Ariel Atom doesn't have much in the way of bodywork or windows, but it makes up for it with insane, face-warping acceleration.

HOW TO SPOT ONE

SCAFFOLDING
There are no body panels on the Atom, just a bunch of pipes to hold it all together.

FACE-BENDING
With masses of power and weighing about the same as a bag of crisps, the Atom accelerates quickly enough to bend the driver's face out of shape...

BIG WING
Not all Atoms have this huge ironing board out the back, but the super-fast V8 and Mugen versions do!

ARIEL ATOM

25 POINTS

ROAD SIGNS

Britain's roadsides are covered by literally millions of signs, ordering motorists to slow down, speed up, stay out of bus lanes, watch out for frogs and make sure their shoelaces are properly tied. OK, we made the last one up. We've gathered together some of the weirder signs on Britain's roads – can you spot them?

BEWARE FALLING ROCKS

2 POINTS

This sign doesn't mean 'hit this ramp at pace and attempt to jump the river'. It means 'swing bridge ahead'. *Top Gear* can confirm that it is best to wait until the bridge is FULLY lowered before attempting to cross, unless you want to end up (a) airborne and (b) in a lot of trouble.

This sign means 'beware falling rocks'. Though we're not quite sure how you're supposed to keep an eye out for falling rocks – which are almost definitely going to attack from above – while also paying attention to the road ahead. Can you cross your eyes?

3 POINTS

SWING BRIDGE AHEAD

26

Warning: Jeremy Clarkson power-testing ahead! Not really. This sign warns that the road ahead may be slippery. This is NOT an invitation to attempt your finest Stig-style powerslides.

SLIPPERY ROAD

2 POINTS

STEEP HILL AHEAD

2 POINTS

This one indicates the steepness of the hill you're just about to go down (or up), not your score in last week's maths test. Don't worry if it's a different percentage to ten – any number at all will score you points! The higher the number, the steeper the hill: if it reads, say, 50%, be prepared for a hairy ride up ahead!

This sign warns of a school crossing up ahead. By which we mean, a crossing used by schoolchildren. Not a school crossing the road. That would be ridiculous. And very slow.

Patrol

2 POINTS

SCHOOL CROSSING

This one means 'watch out for animals in the road ahead'. In this case, it's safe to assume the animals to watch out for are deer. But you can still have the points if you spot the same sign with a cow on it. Or a polar bear. Though that's probably unlikely. In case you're wondering, no, we have no idea how the animals know where to cross. Can deer read?

ANIMALS IN ROAD **2** POINTS

CROSS WINDS **2** POINTS

Beware! Bendy pencils drawing straight lines up ahead! Not really. This sign warns of crosswinds. If you're in a low, sleek car, this sign shouldn't worry you too much. But if you're in something with big, flat sides – like a people-carrier or a lorry – beware of being blown about the road!

WARNING! This sign DOES NOT mean 'plea drive into the water'. That would be very sill and very wet. It's warning that you're close t a big splashy drop into a lot of water. If you' parked near to one of these signs, make sure the driver applies the handbrake properly!

BEWARE WATER **2** POINTS

28

SPEED CAMERAS **2** POINTS

Yes, it's the sign that every driver hates: speed camera ahead! Make sure you obey the speed limit when you see one of these, or you're likely to get a letter in the post from the police...

This sign warns of a ford ahead. That's a ford in the sense of a river running across a road, not an American car with a blue oval badge on its front. But if you spot a Ford in a ford, have an extra few points!

ROADWORKS AHEAD **2** POINTS

FORD AHEAD **2** POINTS

5 POINTS **A FORD IN A FORD**

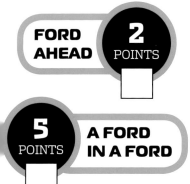

No, it's not a sign warning of a man up ahead who's having difficulty opening his umbrella. This one means 'road works ahead', and it probably means you're going to spend the next few miles crawling along at 5mph...

NO OVERTAKING

2 POINTS

Ah, we know this one. It means 'cup of tea ahead', doesn't it? No? Oh. Actually, this sign means 'dead end ahead'. So if your sat nav is insisting that this road is DEFINITELY the way to London, it's wrong!

Let's have a guess at this one. Only red and black cars allowed on this road? No? Actually, it means 'no overtaking'. Not even if you're in a really, really fast car. Sorry.

DEAD END **2** POINTS

This is definitely not a warning about cars releasing, erm, bottom burps. It actually warns of loose chippings in the road ahead, meaning you're likely to get pelted by gravel kicked up by the car going the other way!

LOOSE CHIPPINGS **2** POINTS

This sign means 'national speed limit applies', and is usually found after an area of roadworks or other speed restrictions. After seeing this, you're permitted to do 60mph on a single lane road, and 70mph on a dual carriageway or motorway. After some long conversations with policemen, *Top Gear* can confirm that this sign is not an invitation to drive as fast as possible...

NATIONAL SPEED LIMIT

1 POINT

This DOES NOT mean 'please attempt to jump over a car on your motorbike'. It means 'no motor vehicles' on this road. So if you're on a horse, cow or bicycle, you're allowed to be there. If you're in a Ferrari, you're about to end up in a lot of trouble...

NO MOTOR VEHICLES

2 POINTS

NO CARAVANS

3 POINTS

We all know how much the British love to take a caravan down the thinnest road ever built and get it stuck, so thankfully the bods at the highways agency have come up with this sign. 'No Caravans'. Whatever!

THE SUPERCARS

They're fast, they're furious, and they're our favourite cars on the planet. Supercars are terrifyingly expensive and made in very limited numbers, so you're unlikely to spot many on our roads... but when you do you'll score big points!

FERRARI

The original and greatest supercar maker. Since 1929, Ferrari has created some of the fastest, most beautiful cars in the history of the universe. You'll be able to recognise a Ferrari because (a) it'll look menacing, low and fast, (b) it'll be making a noise like an angry giant who's just stubbed his toe...

HOW TO SPOT ONE

THE BADGE
Ferraris have a yellow badge with a 'Prancing Horse' logo on, or 'Cavallino Ramparte' in Italian.

THE COLOUR
Ferrari's traditional colour is 'Rosso Corsa', Italian for 'Racing Red'. It's the classic colour of Italian race teams, and definitely worth a few extra points!

ANY FERRARI

20 POINTS

THE NOISE

Ferrari doesn't believe in small, turbocharged engines. Instead, it sticks to V8 and V12 monsters, so keep your ears open as well as your eyes!

A FEW YOU MIGHT SEE

FERRARI 458

Mid-engined V8 Ferrari that's not only gorgeous to look at, but blisteringly fast too. Identify it by its long, sleek headlights!

FERRARI 599

Beautiful supercar with a roaring V12 engine in front. You'll recognise it by its 'flying buttresses' – the aerodynamic bits of bodywork that 'float' either side of the rear window.

FERRARI F40

The scariest Ferrari ever built, and Richard Hammond's favourite supercar of all time. Super-rare, though – only 1,315 were built between 1987 and 1992.

ANY RED FERRARI

30 POINTS

LAMBORGHINI

F errari's arch-rival and creator of some of the most bonkers supercars on the planet. It was Lamborghini that started the trend for mid-engined road cars – with the engine behind, rather than in front of, the driver – and its cars have retained that layout to this day!

HOW TO SPOT ONE

MAD DOORS
Lamborghini has always been the pioneer of crazy doors that open in weird and wonderful fashions. Many of its cars have 'scissor doors', which hinge upwards from the front of the car.

THE BADGE
Lamborghini's logo features a charging bull – in fact, many of its cars are named after famous fighting bulls!

DV·556HA

THE COLOUR
Lambos aren't for drivers who want to remain anonymous. Luminous green and bright yellow are the most popular shades.

34

A FEW YOU MIGHT SEE

LAMBORGHINI GALLARDO
It's called the 'baby Lambo', but there's nothing little about the Gallardo. With razor-sharp edges and a V10 engine, it's impossible to miss!

LAMBORGHINI AVENTADOR
Lambo's latest hypercar has a 691bhp V12 and looks scarier than a mako shark armed with nunchucks!

LAMBORGHINI MURCIELAGO SV
The giant-winged monster driven by Richard Hammond in Abu Dhabi. Good luck spotting one of these: only 186 were ever built!

LAMBO

20 POINTS

ANY GREEN OR YELLOW LAMBO

30 POINTS

AUDI R8

German company Audi has long been famed for making sensible, four-wheel drive saloons (and diesel Le Mans racers), but the R8 is a bit different: a lightning-fast mid-engined supercar to rival the Lamborghini Gallardo and Porsche 911.

HOW TO SPOT ONE

LIGHTS
All-LED headlights glow like evil eyebrows, even in daytime!

SIDEBLADES
Behind the rear edge of the doors, look out for these big scoops that funnel air to the back wheels.

36

THE ROOF

The R8 is made in both coupé and convertible form. As James May discovered, the soft-top provides quite a windy experience!

DON'T CONFUSE IT WITH

The Audi TT. Much smaller, much cheaper, much slower...

AUDI R8 **10** POINTS

15 POINTS **AUDI R8 CONVERTIBLE**

PORSCHE 911

The 911 is the original sports car: first made in 1963 (and originally based on the Beetle, as Jeremy never stops mentioning) it has evolved into one of the best-driving cars on the planet. James and Richard love it, and even Jeremy is finally paying the 911 some begrudging respect...

HOW TO SPOT ONE

ENGINE
Unusually for a sports car, the 911's engine is in the rear, out behind the back wheels. This means there's room for a tiny pair of rear seats, but does occasionally lead to some tail-happy handling!

'TURRET' HEADLIGHTS
911s have (almost) always had round headlights mounted at the front corners of the bonnet like gun barrels.

S·GO 110

DIFFERENT FLAVOURS

The 911 is built in literally dozens of different forms, including a coupé, a convertible, and something in-between called a 'Targa' roof, with a central panel that slides out of the way.

UNIQUE NOISE

The 911 has an unusual 'flat-six' engine that chunters and growls like nothing else on the road! Keep your ears peeled.

DON'T CONFUSE IT WITH...

The Boxster and Cayman, also built by Porsche, look very similar to the 911. But they're a bit smaller and have their engines in the middle instead of at the back. Check the badge carefully!

PORSCHE 911

5 POINTS

39

MASERATI

Think of Maserati as Ferrari's chilled out cousin. Yes, it makes cars that are searingly fast, brilliantly noisy and beautiful, but with a more relaxed attitude than its flighty Italian neighbour. Better still, Maseratis are more common than Ferraris on British roads, so you've got a good chance of seeing one...

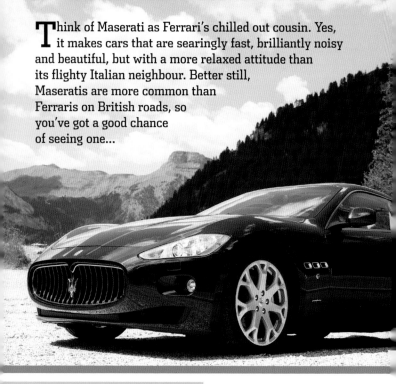

HOW TO SPOT ONE

SLEEK STYLING

Maserati doesn't believe in the sharp angles and creases of Lamborghinis, or giant wings and carbon-fibre bits of Pagani. Watch out for subtle curves.

COLOUR

Maseratis are more understated than most Italian supercars. No bright greens or yellows here, look out for black or dark blue paint...

BADGE
Maserati's emblem is a three-pronged trident, as wielded by Neptune, the Roman god of the sea!

A FEW YOU MIGHT SEE

GRANCABRIO
One of the prettiest convertibles on the planet, with a huge fabric roof. Despite the name, they are rarely driven by grans.

GRANTURISMO
Beautiful V8 coupé that sounds just as delicious as it looks!

QUATTROPORTE
Its name means 'four-door' in Italian, so guess how many doors it has?

ANY MASERATI **10** POINTS

BUGATTI VEYRON

The fastest car in the world, ever. With a 1000bhp 16-cylinder engine and a top speed in excess of 250mph, you'll be very lucky ever to spot a Veyron. Not only because it'll be gone in a flash, but also because it's super-rare: costing over a million pounds, only a few hundred have ever been built.

HOW TO SPOT ONE

HORSESHOE GRILLE
The grille between the Veyron's 'eyes' is shaped like an upside-down horseshoe.

BADGE
The backwards 'E' and 'B' on the Veyron represent the initials of Ettore Bugatti, the company's founder.

SPEED

With a 0-60mph time of just over two seconds, you'll need a sharp pair of eyes to keep tabs on the warp-speed Veyron.

SUPER SPORT

In 2010, clearly deciding the 254mph Veyron wasn't quick enough, Bugatti introduced the upgraded 'Super Sport' version, with an extra 200bhp and a top speed of 268mph. You can spot the Super Sport by the big ducts on its roof that funnel air into the giant engine...

BUGATTI VEYRON

100 POINTS

MERCEDES-BENZ SLS AMG

Mercedes's 'AMG' tuning department once confined itself to cooking up hotter versions of the company's road cars. But in 2010, Mercedes let the German boffins build their first-ever supercar, and the result was the giant, gull-winged SLS, which wrapped a bellowing 6.2-litre V8 engine in a mad, retro body.

44

HOW TO SPOT ONE

LONG, LONG BONNET
With the huge engine in front of the driver but behind the line of the front wheels, the SLS's bonnet seems to stretch on forever.

GULLWINGS
The SLS's doors hinge up from the roof like a bird raising its wings. Not so easy to close if you've got short arms!

HUGE BADGE
That giant three-pointed Mercedes star on the front is a bit of a giveaway.

DON'T CONFUSE IT WITH...
The Mercedes SL, which is much smaller, cheaper and nowhere near as noisy!

MERCEDES SLS

20 POINTS

PAGANI ZONDA

Is this the maddest supercar ever made? It just might be. The spaceship-like, futuristic Zonda was first built in 1999, and continued to gain more power and speed all the way until it was finally retired in 2011. Just a few dozen were ever built, making this one of the rarest supercar spots on the planet.

HOW TO SPOT ONE

CARBON FIBRE

The Zonda is built almost completely of carbon fibre, meaning it's not only incredibly strong but lightweight too.

46

FOUR EXHAUSTS
Look out for that big circular tailpipe with a stack of four exhausts in the middle!

THE NOISE
With a screaming V12 engine borrowed from Mercedes' AMG division, you'll probably be able to hear the Zonda before you see it!

PAGANI ZONDA

80 POINTS

ALFA ROMEO 8C

Jeremy described the 8C as 'the best-looking car ever made', and for once he might be right. With classical curves and a roaring V8 engine, the sleek Alfa is a real treat for both eyes and ears. Just a pity most of us will never see one: only 500 were ever built, between 2007 and 2009.

HOW TO SPOT ONE

CURVACEOUS
The 8C has more swoops and curves than a map of the Nürburgring!

FLAT BACK
The 8C doesn't have a long, pointed tail, but instead a cut-off backside with a pair of round rear lamps in either corner.

THE ROOF
Was built in both hard-top and convertible form.
Unfortunately both are INCREDIBLY rare!

50 POINTS

ALFA ROMEO 8C

49

KOENIGSEGG

The maddest thing to come out of Sweden since, erm... ever! Capable of top speeds close to 250mph, Koeniseggs are among the fastest road cars ever made, and are also some of the rarest – just a couple have ever been spotted in the UK. In fact, the only thing more difficult than actually seeing a Koenigsegg on the road... is spelling the name of the company!

HOW TO SPOT ONE

BIG WING

After Stig crashed a CCX into the tyre wall on the *Top Gear* track, later cars were given the '*Top Gear*' wing...

50

SIX LIGHTS
The rear of the CCX has two strips of three lights. Tough to miss!

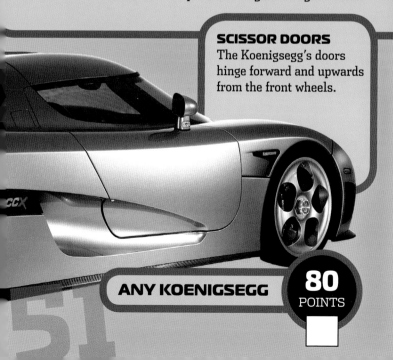

SCISSOR DOORS
The Koenigsegg's doors hinge forward and upwards from the front wheels.

ANY KOENIGSEGG

80 POINTS

51

NISSAN GT-R

The GT-R is one of the fastest cars ever built, smashing 0-60mph in three seconds flat thanks to its 500bhp twin-turbo engine and all-wheel drive. In fact, the GT-R is so quick and so grippy that it nearly snapped Jeremy's neck when he tested it on the race track! But despite all its pace, the GT-R is half the price of most supercars... so there's a good chance you'll see one on the road...

HOW TO SPOT ONE

REAR LIGHTS
Four round lamps at the back, right above the huge tailpipes.

REAR SEATS
They're only tiny but, unlike most supercars, the GT-R does actually have chairs in the back.

EVIL EYES

The GT-R isn't a beautiful supercar, but it's a very effective one! Look out for its long headlights and big, square front grille.

NISSAN GT-R

10 POINTS

DOGS IN CARS

Score points for spotting man's best friend taking a road trip with his owner. But how many points depends on where the plucky pooch is sitting...

DOG IN THE BOOT

The correct, safe place for dogs to travel. But a bit boring. If there's more than one dog there, add another point for each one!

1
POINT
per dog

3
POINTS

DOG ON THE FRONT SEAT

Now, this is where Rover wants to be. Sitting up front, watching the road ahead, changing the radio station if he doesn't like the music...

5
POINTS

DOG WITH HEAD OUT THE WINDOW

Look at him, the floppy-eared buffoon! Look how happy he is!

DOG DRIVING

No, no, no. This is bad and dangerous and will probably end in a crash. If you see this, is it best to alert the authorities immediately. It is very unlikely that this dog has a valid driving licence.

0
POINTS

THE HOT HATCHES

Start with a basic, practical, grown-up hatchback. Then stuff it with a load more power, sportier suspension, a few wings and a few other go-faster bits. What do you end up with? That's right, a hot hatch. They're small, they're fizzy, and they're among *Top Gear*'s very favourite cars. Here's a few to watch out for on the road...

VOLKSWAGEN GOLF GTI

The Golf GTI was the original hot hatch. Introduced wayyyy back in 1976, it started life producing just over 100bhp – which doesn't sound like much, but then again it did weigh only 800kg! Since then, there have been SIX generations of Golf GTI. Here they all are:

Mk1: 1975-1984
Mk2: 1984-1987
Mk3: 1987-1998
Mk4: 1998-2004
Mk5: 2004-2009
Mk6: 2009-2012
Mk7: 2012-present

Though it's changed a great deal over the years, the GTI has a few 'signature' features...

56

TARTAN INTERIOR
Many GTIs are upholstered with this traditional Scottish pattern.

RED, WHITE AND BLACK
The most traditional Golf GTI colours.

COOL WHEELS
Golf GTIs have always had good-looking alloys...

5
POINTS

FORD FOCUS ST/RS

Ford has a long and glorious history of making fast, affordable cars, and its hotted-up Focuses are among the best hot hatches in the world. There are actually quite a few fast Focuses worth keeping an eye out for...

FORD FOCUS ST
Ford made two generations of Focus ST: the first between 2002 and 2005, and the second between 2005 and 2011.

HOW TO SPOT ONE

BIG ARCHES
STs have 'flared' wheel arches, making the car look wider and more muscular.

ST BADGE
Stands for 'Sport Technologies'. Not 'Stig Tested'...

ORANGE PAINT
The ST's 'signature' colour. But blue and white were also popular...

ORANGE FOCUS ST

5 POINTS   FOCUS ST

10 POINTS

58

FORD FOCUS RS

This is even faster and even rarer than the ST, so worth even more points! There are two generations of RS to look out for, and they're both devilishly quick.

MK1 FOCUS RS

Just two thousand of the first-generation RSs were produced between 2002 and 2003, all painted dark blue. Look for the 'RS' badge on the boot!

'Mk1' FOCUS RS

10 POINTS

MK2 FOCUS RS

The second-generation Focus was only available in green, blue and white, and produced a mighty 300bhp from its turbocharged five-cylinder engine. Here's how to spot it:

BIG WING
Helps keep those rear tyres pressing down on the road.

BONNET VENTS
Prevents the turbo engine from overheating.

15 POINTS

BIG MOUTH
Looks like an angry shark...

FORD FOCUS RS500

The ultimate Focus spot is the super-limited edition RS500. Based on the MkII Focus RS above, just 500 of these cars were built, all with a massive 345bhp and a scary, non-shiny 'matte black' paintjob. You'll need quick eyes to keep tabs on this one: it's the most powerful front-wheel drive car in the world!

FORD FOCUS RS500

20 POINTS

59

RENAULT-SPORT CLIO

Unusually for hot hatches, the fast versions of the usually-quite-boring Renault Clio don't have turbochargers. But don't think this means they're a bit dull. Quite the opposite: the fizzy little Clio was even good enough to impress James May when he drove it from Lecce to Monaco on *Top Gear's* Hot Hatch Challenge!

HOW TO SPOT ONE

CLIO 197

BIG REAR DIFFUSER
Black plastic moulding helps produce downforce and keep the back tyres on the tarmac!

BIG WHEELS
Normal Clios come with small, dull rims. The Clio 197s are huge twelve-spoke jobs... some cars even had black wheels!

COLOUR
Many Clio 197s were painted blue or yellow... but not all!

CLIO 200

BLACK BUMPER
No matter what colour the car, all Clio 200s have a 'mouth' painted in shiny black.

BRIGHT COLOURS
You'll see Clio 200s in many different colours, but most popular are bright yellow and Kermit-the-Frog green!

SWEATY DRIVER
The hardcore 'Cup' version of the Clio 200 didn't even have air conditioning, so watch out for perspiring passengers on a hot day!

HV09 YFR

CLIO 200

5 POINTS

VAUXHALL ASTRA VXR

The Astra VXR isn't a subtle, sophisticated hot hatch. In fact, it's fightier than a pit bull with a bad temper! Built between 2005 and 2010, it made a whopping 237bhp from its 2.0-litre turbocharged engine, and was renowned for its rather wriggly handling!

HOW TO SPOT ONE

CENTRAL EXHAUST
VXR has a single tailpipe, just below its rear number plate. Quite a lot of noise emerges from here.

THREE DOORS ONLY
There was never a five-door Astra VXR produced.

NO GREYS OR BROWNS
Red, white and blue were the most popular VXR colours.

ASTRA VXR

5 POINTS

HONDA CIVIC TYPE R

To date, Honda has built three generations of Civic Type R. The first two – made between 1996 and 2005 – were quite conventional-looking. But the third– made from 2007 to 2010 – was entirely bonkers: it looked like a modified spaceship! That's the one we want you to look out for...

HOW TO SPOT ONE

REAR WING
Cuts straight across the back windscreen.

WHITE
It's the traditional Civic Type R colour, but red and black were popular too.

TYPE R
Look out for this red badge on the bottom right-hand side of the boot lid.

ASTRA VXR:

5 POINTS

ABARTH 500

It might be small, but the hot 500 – as thrashed around Monaco by Richard Hammond – isn't to be trifled with! Though it starts life as a humble Fiat 500, by the end of its transformation into a scrappy hot hatch, the fizzy 500 doesn't wear a single Fiat badge – it's actually classed as an Abarth instead...

HOW TO SPOT ONE

LOTS OF SCORPIONS
The scorpion is Abarth's symbol, and it's all over the little 500!

SOFT OR HARD TOP
The Abarth 500 is available either as a coupé, or with a fabric roof that rolls back.

RED WING MIRRORS
They're not compulsory, but most Abarth 500s have bright red wing mirror surrounds.

STICKERS

Again, they're not standard issue, but you'll spot plenty of Abarth 500s with decals between their front and rear wheels.

10 POINTS

ABARTH 500:

65

ANIMALS ON THE ROAD

Roads are meant for cars, bikes and other wheeled machines, but occasionally our furry friends choose to ignore this. Out in the countryside, it's not unusual to spot a few animals lumbering happily along the tarmac...

IMPORTANT SCORING NOTES

1. The creature has to be on the road itself, not in a field near the road. Or a zoo. That's cheating.
2. No extra points for spotting more than one of the same animal: you don't score a hundred points if you encounter a herd of sheep crossing the road!

HORSES

One point if there's a rider atop it, three points if not. Make sure you give horses a wide berth in a car!

HORSE WITH RIDER

1 POINT

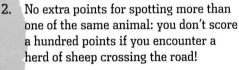

HORSE WITHOUT RIDER

3 POINTS

COW

Quite a common sight on rural roads. A bit less common on urban high streets! Treat them with respect or they'll make a big beefy mess of your car.

COW **2** POINTS

SHEEP

If you're in deepest Wales, it's almost certain you'll see a sheep on the tarmac at some point. In really remote areas, sheep are more common than cars!

SHEEP **1** POINT

LLAMA

OK, you're a bit less likely to see a llama on the road than a cow or a sheep. But with a few thousand kept by farmers in the UK, it's still possible!

| LLAMA | **5** POINTS |

BLUE WHALE

Oh dear. Something's gone very wrong here. If you spot the world's largest animal on the road, best call all the emergency services. And the *Guinness Book of Records*. And your doctor.

100 POINTS | BLUE WHALE

ELEPHANT

This seems really quite unlikely. But you never know: maybe there's been a breakout from the local zoo?

ELEPHANT **30** POINTS

69

AMERICAN MUSCLE

They're big, they're brash and they're Richard Hammond's favourites. Yes, they're American muscle cars and, though they're a rare sight on British roads, they'll guarantee you big points if you spot 'em!

FORD MUSTANG

First built in the early 1960s, the Mustang was one of the very first muscle cars and remains Hammond's dream machine: in fact, he owns a 1968 GT390!

HOW TO SPOT ONE

BADGE

Instead of the normal 'Blue Oval' Ford badge, Mustangs feature a galloping horse on their badges. The Shelby versions – which are even hotter than normal Mustangs – have a snake on them.

SMOKING REAR TYRES

Muscle cars don't believe in safe, sensible four-wheel drive. So don't be surprised to see a Mustang burning up its rear wheels!

TWO DOORS

If it's got rear doors, it ain't a Mustang...

FORD MUSTANG

10 POINTS

CHEVROLET CAMARO

F or the last forty-five years, the Camaro has gone bumper-to-bumper with its arch-enemy, the Ford Mustang. Like the Mustang, it's a blocky, no-nonsense muscle car and, like the Mustang, it usually has a shouty V8 under its bonnet. But be warned: in the UK it's an even rarer sight than the Ford!

HOW TO SPOT ONE

ORANGE PAINT
OK, so not ALL Camaros are painted 'Inferno Orange', but it's the traditional shade for Chevy's muscle car...

RACING STRIPES
Again, they won't be on EVERY Camaro, but watch out for a pair of stripes running the length of the body.

BIG HIPS
Look out for these wide, high flares above the rear wheels.

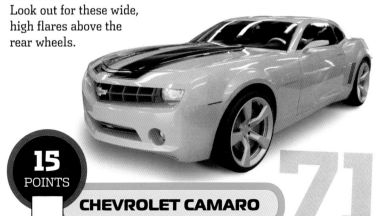

15 POINTS

CHEVROLET CAMARO

71

DODGE CHARGER

It's common for manufacturers to revive their greatest hits of old, but how often do they add a couple of extra doors? That's what happened with the Charger: the original muscle car of the Sixties and Seventies was a two-door coupé, but the modern version – introduced in 2005 – is a four-door!

HOW TO SPOT ONE

REAR DOORS
Unlike most muscle cars, the modern Charger has back doors...

'CROSS' GRILLE
Look out for large vertical and horizontal stripes across modern Charger's front grille.

SHARP EDGES
Sharp crease runs from the rear door handles to the tail lights.

DODGE CHARGER

15 POINTS

DODGE VIPER

The Viper isn't a conventional muscle car. For a start, it's a two-seater sports car rather than a coupé with a second row of seats. Secondly, it has a V10 rather than the traditional V8 engine. But for its brutish power and ability to demolish a set of rear tyres in seconds, it earns its place in the *Spotter's Guide*'s muscle section!

20 POINTS

☐

DODGE VIPER

HOW TO SPOT ONE

HUUUUUUUGE BONNET
There's an EIGHT-LITRE V10 engine under there, no wonder it's long!

BIG MOUTH
Though its design has evolved since the first version was introduced in 1992, all Vipers have featured the same curvy front end and large, gaping grille.

TERRIFIED DRIVER
The Viper doesn't have much in the way of 'driver aids' – expect to see the driver clinging on tight!

73

BUMPER STICKERS

For some people, their choice of car doesn't say enough about them. No, they want other road-users to know that they love Manchester United, or kayaking, or Stilton, or dachshunds, or... actually, any one of a million different things. Usually stuck on the back bumper, down by the number plate, some bumper stickers are funny, some are thoughtful and some are plain stupid. We've cooked up a bunch of bumper stickers suitable for *Top Gear* – you won't spot these on the road, but have a point for every car you spot with a bumper sticker!

LAND ROVER

RCC 127

I ♥ DUCKS

HAMSTER ON BOARD

ANY BUMPER STICKER

1 POINT

PRESENTERS

Y̲ou can see them on telly just about every day but spotting *Top Gear*'s famous quartet in the wild is rather trickier. Shy and retiring (well, one of them, anyhow), they're rarely seen travelling on foot, preferring the safety, speed and privacy of a powerful motor vehicle. That's why you'll score HUGE points for seeing them in real life!

JEREMY CLARKSON

T̲he noisy, tall one from *Top Gear*. When not powersliding around the *Top Gear* test track, Jeremy can usually be found in the Oxfordshire village of Chipping Norton, where he relaxes by shouting and jumping Rolls-Royces into the local lido.

HOW TO SPOT ONE

JEANS
Legs will be clad in denim.

VERY TALL
No one knows exactly how tall Jeremy is, as a ruler long enough to measure him has not yet been invented!

SHOUTING
Will probably be making loud noises from the mouth region.

SMELLS
Slightly of burning rubber, after spending too many years destroying tyres on power tests at the *Top Gear* track.

ONE JEREMY CLARKSON

100 POINTS

RICHARD HAMMOND

The other noisy one from *Top Gear*. Frequently spotted in the darkest depths of Wales, either blazing around in a classicAmerican muscle car or desperately trying to fix a creaking old Land Rover with a combination of spanners and shouting.

HOW TO SPOT ONE

WHITE TEETH
Completely natural, of course.

DIET
If it's eating anything (a) foreign, (b) slimy or (c) with a funny name, it is NOT a Hammond. Hammonds prefer a meat-and-potato-based diet.

HAIRCUT
Changes week-by-week. Sometimes shaggy, sometimes fluffy, sometimes spiky...

100 POINTS

ONE RICHARD HAMMOND

77

JAMES MAY

Or Captain Slow, as he's also known. If he's not pottering around near the *Top Gear* studio complaining about the ride quality of modern sports cars, James will probably be found in a garage in the Hammersmith area of London, carefully fixing an old motorbike while explaining the intricacies of limited-slip differentials to anyone who'll listen...

HOW TO SPOT ONE

HAIR
Lots of it, definitely not brushed.

A FLOWERY SHIRT
Probably bright. Maybe with a bit of pink on it.

PROBABLY LOST
May be asking directions. Probably to the pub.

78

JAMES MAY

100 POINTS

THE STIG

Some say he's invisible to radar. Some say he's never been seen in the same room as Kristin Scott Thomas. Some say that, on Thursdays, he's often found in DIY shops in the Middlesbrough area, buying hundreds of self-tapping screws. All we know is... he's called The Stig and he's one of the rarest spots in the whole of this book...

HOW TO SPOT ONE

SMELL
Unholy. Like an fusty old cat wrapped in bacon.

NOISE
None whatsoever. As silent as a very, very quiet library.

SUIT
White. Any other colour and it's not the Stig... it's an imposter!

POSTURE
Either (a) arms crossed, looking unimpressed or (b) behind the wheel of a fast car, setting a blistering lap of the *Top Gear* track.

WHITE STIG

200 POINTS

WEIRD STUFF

Some cars are fast. Some cars are beautiful. And some are just a bit... odd. If there's nothing speedy or stunning to spot on the road, keep a look out for these freaks and oddballs from around the globe. Be warned, though – some might cause lasting damage to your eyes!

DAIHATSU COPEN

The Copen is a Japanese kei car, built to strict regulations governing size and power. This explains why it's (a) rather tiny and (b) rather slow. But surely the Copen can't blame kei car regulations for the fact that it looks like Noddy's Toytown car?

HOW TO SPOT ONE

FOLDING HARD-TOP
The Copen's metal roof flips down into the boot, transforming it into a convertible.

NOT VERY FAST
With a 68bhp engine and a 0-60mph time of ten seconds, don't expect to see the Copen speeding off into the distance!

VERY SMALL
The Copen stands just 120cm high!

DAIHATSU COPEN

5 POINTS

FIAT QUBO/PEUGEOT BIPPER/CITROËN NEMO

Many manufacturers have converted their panel vans into cheap people-movers. But never have the results been quite so ugly as the Fiat Qubo, Peugeot Bipper and Citroën Nemo – identical cars with different names and badges...

QUBO/BIPPER/NEMO

5 POINTS

HOW TO SPOT ONE

HUGE CHIN
Look out for that big, square chin jutting out from beneath the headlights.

SLIDING REAR DOORS
Slide towards the boot to provide a welcome escape for back-seat passengers!

BARE METAL
No comfy leather or cozy cushions inside – these MPVs are barely more luxurious than the vans they're based on!

SSANGYONG RODIUS

It's called the Rodius and it is indeed odious. Korean manufacturer Ssangyong isn't famous for making beautiful cars, but the Rodius is ugly even by the firm's own low standards. We can only guess that the designer responsible for the front of the car never met the one responsible for the back!

HOW TO SPOT ONE

WEIRD BOOT
Surely this was glued on as an afterthought?

SAD FACE
Well, you'd have an expression like that too if you looked like this!

GIGANTIC
Though it's sold as a seven-seater in the UK, the Rodius is huge enough to be offered as an ELEVEN-seater abroad!

SSANGYONG RODIUS

5 POINTS

82

MITSUBISHI i

Like the Daihatsu Copen, the i is a 'Kei car', which means it's tiny and has a dinky engine. In fact, some don't have an engine at all, running on all-electric power instead!

HOW TO SPOT ONE

BUG EYES
The i's motor is in its boot, so there's no bonnet to speak of, just a pair of insect-like headlights above the front wheels!

SILENT RUNNING
Most are petrol-powered, but there's an electric version too, called the i-MiEV. It runs completely silently, so it might sneak up on you!

NARROW
Measuring barely a metre and a half across, the i can sneak through even the narrowest gaps in traffic.

MITSUBISHI i

10 POINTS

83

RENAULT WIND

Yes, it's really called the Wind. No laughing, you at the back. Based on the Twingo, the Clio is a tiny, tinny two-seat convertible with a folding roof that's much more complicated than it needs to be. And it's called the Wind. The Wind. For some reason Renault never sold very many in the UK...

HOW TO SPOT ONE

FLIPPY ROOF
The Wind's hard top flips away from the top of the windscreen and under the boot compartment.

BIG BUM
To provide space to stow the roof, the Wind has a HUGE bottom. In fact, its backside is nearly as tall as it is wide!

FANGS
Beneath its headlights, the Wind has these little triangular vents. Don't they look like pointy teeth?

RENAULT
WIND

10
POINTS

84

SMART ROADSTER

It's one of the smallest convertibles on the road, and – though it really shouldn't be – the Roadster is actually quite cool. Powered by a tiny three-cylinder engine, the Smart Roadster isn't especially fast, but it's a fizzy little customer!

HOW TO SPOT ONE

IT'S ALL YELLOW
The Smart Roadster was available in other colours, but the majority were painted yellow...

LOOK DOWN
Measuring just 120cm in height, it's easy to miss the tiny Smart Roadster. Check down at knee-height!

TWO-SEATER
No space in the back for people. Or shopping. Or anything, in fact...

SMART ROADSTER

10 POINTS

TOYOTA IQ

As its name suggests, the iQ is very clever, packed with the sort of innovative engineering that impresses boffins like James May. It's also tiny: though there's seating inside for three full-size humans (plus one more with no legs), it measures under three metres in length!

HOW TO SPOT ONE

FUNNY FACE
Is this the expression of a car that's just caught a whiff of a bad smell?

WIDE WHEELS
The iQ's wheels are pushed right out to the very corners of its body: nice and easy to park.

'WRAPAROUND' REAR WINDOW
The iQ's rear screen seems to curve out onto the car's flanks.

86

TOYOTA IQ

5 POINTS

ASTON MARTIN CYGNET

A Toyota iQ with an Aston badge on the front, a load of posh leather inside... and a £30,000 price tag!

20 POINTS

ASTON MARTIN CYGNET

NISSAN JUKE

The basic concept of the Juke isn't too weird: a small SUV with five seats and the option of four-wheel drive. But look at its weird face! Nissan describes the Juke's design as 'distinctive' – we can't argue with that!

HOW TO SPOT ONE

STRANGE LIGHTS
Long, swept-back clusters on top of the bonnet, two big round bulbs down by the grille... what's going on here?

NOT SO BIG
It looks chunky, but the Juke is deceptively small – in fact, it's barely longer than a Ford Fiesta!

TRENDY TAIL LIGHTS
Nissan calls the Juke's rear lights 'boomerangs'...

NISSAN JUKE

3 POINTS

DAIHATSU MATERIA

Yes, it's the car that Jeremy tested against an Ascari A10. It might not look or sound as good as the 625bhp British sports car, but the blocky Materia is far more practical: it has three more seats than the Ascari... and it's a few hundred thousand pounds cheaper, too! We know which one we'd back in a drag race, though...

HOW TO SPOT ONE

BOXY
Forget sleek supercar curves: the Materia is almost completely cuboid!

LOW LIGHTS
Look out for the rear lights plonked just above the wheels.

NOT VERY FAST
With its 1.5-litre engine making just 100bhp, the Materia won't trouble an Ascari in a track battle!

DAIHATSU MATERIA

10 POINTS

89

NISSAN FIGARO

I t looks like a product of the 1950s, but the Figaro was actually built in the 1990s. Some retro cars – like the Fiat 500 or the Alfa Romeo 8C – manage to combine looking old-school and cool, but the Figaro is as unfashionable as a nasty bout of head lice...

HOW TO SPOT ONE

WHITE ROOF
Most Figaros were painted in unpleasant shades of pink or green, but their roofs were always white.

SILLY FACE
Round headlights, a funny little oval grille – it's not the most handsome car in the world, is it?

GOING SLOWLY
The Figaro has a 1.0-litre, 75bhp engine. Expect to see it being overtaken by tractors. And cows.

NISSAN FIGARO

5 POINTS

RIVA G-WIZ

RIVA G-WIZ

3 POINTS

Probably the worst car on sale in the UK. The G-Wiz is a tiny electric vehicle that's so rickety and slow that it doesn't even qualify as a car: it's technically classed as a 'quadricycle'!

FOUR SEATS (TECHNICALLY)
Yes, the G-Wiz has rear seats. You'd have to be pretty cruel to make someone sit in them, though!

SILENT RUNNING
Running on electric power alone, you won't hear the G-Wiz sneaking up on you until it's too late!

STOPPED WORKING?
The G-Wiz's batteries can manage just a few dozen miles before needing to be recharged, so don't be surprised to see one stopped by the side of the road, out of juice...

91

CITROËN 2CV

The 2CV is Citroën's best-selling car ever: between 1948 and 1990, over FIVE MILLION were built around the world! The original 2CV produced just two horsepower, but was capable of being driven across a ploughed field with a basket of eggs on its passenger seat... without breaking any!

HOW TO SPOT ONE

UPSIDE-DOWN PRAM
The 2CV has a very distinctive profile – like a baby's pram turned on its roof!

LOTS OF HOOPS
The 2CV was designed as a series of 'croquet hoop' shapes: one for the roof and two for the front and rear wheel arches.

RUST
2CVs were built as cheaply as possible, so don't be surprised to see a bit of rust and a few dents!

CITROËN 2CV

5 POINTS

LADA NIVA

First built in 1977, the Niva is Russia's most famous off-roader. Though it's tiny by modern standards, and about as luxurious as a prison cell, it's almost indestructible. Very few Nivas were brought to the UK, but you can bet that they're all still rattling around!

HOW TO SPOT ONE

STRAIGHT LINES
The Niva was never fashionable. It's small and square and almost impossible to break.

NO FRILLS
Don't expect sat navs or leather or even air conditioning; the Niva is as basic as a car can be.

OFF-ROAD
It might not be high-tech, but the Niva is capable of driving almost anywhere. Don't be surprised to see one in the middle of a field!

LADA NIVA

10 POINTS

93

FIAT MULTIPLA

Is this the ugliest car ever made? The original Fiat Multipla, first built in 1999, featured a second set of lights above the normal headlights, right at the base of the windscreen. It looked like something from the bottom of the ocean. In 2004, Fiat got rid of the Multipla's awful extra lights, but it's the original you'll have to spot if you want points!

HOW TO SPOT ONE

EVIL EYES
Yuck, who put those there? It looks like one car has been dropped on top of another!

THREE SEATS
The Multipla had three seats up front rather than the usual two.

LOTS OF GLASS
Multipla passengers got a nice view of the outside world... and, even better, didn't have to behold the ugliness of the car they were in!

FIAT MULTIPLA

NOT THIS ONE
See? The facelifted Multipla looks pretty much normal. No points if you spot this one...

PERSONALISED NUMBER PLATES

*T*op Gear has never really understood personalized number plates, but they seem to be very popular. But how exactly do they work? Well, most British number plates follow one of these formats:

ABC123D
Three letters, up to three numbers, one letter.

A123BCD
One letter, up to three numbers, three letters.

AB12CDE
Two letters, two numbers, three letters.

Within these rules, canny drivers have spent years figuring out how to use these basic combinations to 'spell' words. Personalised number plates often rely on numbers looking similar to letters – for example, 1 looks like I, 2 looks like Z, 3 looks like E, and so on. So James May might drive a car with a number plate like this:

CPT 5IOW

Of course, he doesn't. But would Clarkson like one like this?

J3ZZA

And how about this one for Richard?

HAM57A

Drivers have used dozens of devious tricks in pursuit of their perfect plate: two ls with a well-placed black screw in the middle will make an 'H', while an O with a yellow or white screw at the top suddenly becomes a 'U'.

To get you used to spotting personalized plates, we've cooked up a few that might be suitable for *Top Gear*. Once you've worked out what they all say, keep your eyes peeled for real-life personalized plates on the road!

PERSONALIZED NUMBER PLATE

1
POINT

PAINTJOBS

Grey, silver, orange, blue, even yellow... they're all a bit boring, aren't they? To score points, you'll have to spot one of these REALLY weird paintjobs.

MATTE BLACK

Don't be fooled, this isn't a dusty car, just one covered in matte paint! Often referred to as 'flat', matte paint doesn't reflect as much light as normal paintwork. It looks evil but, as Jeremy discovered when he tested the M3 Competition Pack, it does have a couple of problems: you can't polish it or even take it to a car wash!

MATTE BLACK CAR

10 POINTS

CHROME

Shiny silver cars are ten a penny, but chrome paintjobs are rather rarer. Favoured by celebrities wanting to show off, chromed cars look as if they're wrapped in a huge, warped mirror!

CHROME CAR

10 POINTS

MULTICOLOUR

Why have just one paint colour when you could have two, three, four or more? Some cars – like the Bugatti Veyron or Abarth 500C – look pretty sharp with a two-tone paintjob. Others – like the Polo Harlequin – look a complete mess (yes, it was really designed like that!).

TWO PAINT COLOURS — **2** POINTS

THREE PAINT COLOURS — **2** POINTS

But even cars that weren't designed to be multicoloured sometimes end up so. If you see a car with non-matching bits, chances are it's been in a crash and the owner couldn't find the right colour of replacement panel!

MORE THAN THREE — **2** POINTS

RACING STRIPES
On a muscle car like the Ford Mustang, racing stripes can look super-cool. But on a 1.0-litre Citroën Saxo, they just look a bit daft. Whatever Hammond might tell you, racing stripes scientifically DO NOT make a car go faster!

ONE STRIPE — **1** POINTS

2 POINTS — **TWO STRIPES**

THE THREE-WHEELERS

Most cars, as you will have noticed, have four wheels. This is a good number of wheels if you like your vehicle not to tip over when going round corners. But a few cars survive with just three wheels – how many can you spot on the roads?

RELIANT ROBIN

Probably your best chance of spying a three-wheeler. Built in England between 1973 and 2002, the Robin technically qualified as a motorcycle, so was cheaper to tax and insure.

HOW TO SPOT ONE

ON ITS ROOF?
As Jeremy found out, it is very easy to 'roll' a Reliant Robin. If you spot a car upside-down with three wheels waggling in the air, it's probably a Robin!

LIGHTWEIGHT
The Robin was made of fiberglass. Though this wasn't very good news in a crash, it did at least mean that it was nice and light to roll back onto its feet if you'd accidentally tipped it over!

CAN-AM SPYDER

What do you get if you cross a motorbike with a quad? The Can-Am Spyder, that's what – a bike-engined monster with two wheels at the front and one at the back.

CAN-AM SPYDER

15 POINTS

HOW TO SPOT ONE

HELMET
It's windy on board the Spyder – not to mention quite dangerous – so expect its driver to be wearing a 'lid'!

SPEEDY
Its engine only makes 105bhp, but don't be fooled: the Can-Am is truly quick. It'll do 0-60mph in under five seconds and 120mph flat out!

UNMISSABLE
The Can-Am's signature colour is bright yellow. If you don't like being centre of attention, this probably isn't the machine for you!

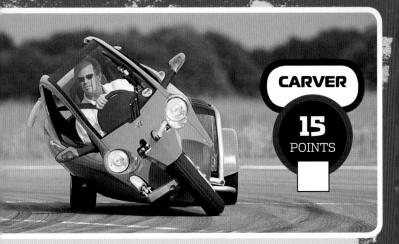

CARVER

Motorbikes have two wheels. Cars have four. Motorbikes tilt when they go round corners. Cars don't. So what does that make the Carver? This three-wheeler leans into corners like a motorcycle, but has a windscreen and a pair of rear wheels like a car. Whatever it is, Jeremy described it 'the most fun you can have'...

HOW TO SPOT ONE

TILTING
When being driven fast, the Carver tilts towards the inside of a corner: in other words, it'll lean left while going round a left-hander.

NARROW
Even at its widest point, the Carver measures just 130cm across.

MOTORBIKE FRONT WHEEL
The Carver's front wheel has been borrowed straight from the world of superbikes, right down to that fender!

PEEL P50

It's the smallest car ever made, and Jeremy's favourite way of getting around the office! Originally built between 1962 and 1965, the Peel P50 is powered by a tiny 49cc engine producing just 4bhp, and has a top speed of just 38mph. Measuring just 137cm from nose to tail and weighing just 59kg, it's the shortest and lightest car ever to go into production.

COLOUR
P50s were only made in red, white or blue.

NO GOING BACK
With no reverse gear, the only way to make a Peel go backwards was to get out and push it!

PEEL P50

15 POINTS

INDOORS
The Peel is so dinky that, as Jeremy found out, it can easily be driven indoors! Keep an eye out in your school corridors...

SPEED AND SAFETY CAMERAS

A long with traffic wardens and the G-Wiz, they're probably the most hated things on the road. Every year, more and more cameras pop up on Britain's streets, so you've got a good chance of spotting one! If you see a camera, whoever's driving will probably appreciate you pointing it out...

GATSO

Probably the most common type of speed cameras, GATSOs are always painted yellow, and point in the direction that cars are travelling: in other words, they take a photo of the back of a speeding car.

1 POINTS

GATSO

SPECS

You'll often see these when roadworks are taking place on a motorway. SPECS cameras measure a car's average speed over a certain distance: one camera takes a photo at the start of the stretch of road, and another takes a photo when you've reached the end of it. The system then calculates your speed based on how long it took you to drive the distance – if you went quicker than the speed limit, you'll get a ticket!

SPECS — **1** POINTS

TRAFFIC LIGHT CAMERAS

These aren't painted yellow, so they're more difficult to spot. They're positioned on junctions to spot drivers who jump red lights, so keep an eye out at busy intersections!

TRAFFIC LIGHT CAMERA — **1** POINTS

MOBILE SPEED TRAP

You never know where these are going to crop up! In some parts of the country, police are permitted to 'clock' drivers using mobile speed-measuring devices. Sometimes they'll be poking from the back of a van, sometimes they'll simply be standing by the side of the road with a laser gun. As they could be hiding literally anywhere, there's only one way to avoid being caught by a mobile speed trap: don't go over the limit!

MOBILE SPEED TRAP — **1** POINTS

HATS

Unless you're (a) a racing driver, (b) crossing the desert in a convertible or (c) crossing the Arctic in a convertible, there's no need to wear a hat while driving. But many still do. And you can get points for spotting them. There's just one very important rule here: you don't get any points for baseball caps – proper hats only! Here, the boys model just some of the headwear that could score you points...

HATS **10** POINTS

THE ORIGINALS

In recent years, it's become fashionable for manufacturers to wheel out updated versions of their biggest hits through history. Here, you can score points for spotting the original versions...

OLD MINI

The original Mini first arrived on British roads in 1959. Measuring just three metres in length, and boasting front-wheel drive and unusual rubbery suspension, it was a revolutionary car. The Mini  was so successful that it remained in production in Britain for over forty years, selling over 1.5 million cars around the world!

HOW TO SPOT ONE

TINY
Only 120cm high, the Mini is just about small enough to park in the boot of most modern cars!

ROUND HEADLIGHTS
Simple circular 'eyes' – cheap and cheerful!

UNION JACK ON THE ROOF
Not EVERY Mini had the British flag painted on top, but plenty did. Have 3 more points if you spot it...

OLD MINI

15 POINTS

OLD FIAT 500

First produced in 1957, the Fiat 500 – or 'Cinquecento' in Italian – was one of the first true city cars. With an air-cooled engine in its boot, the 500 was truly tiny – it was less than three metres long and weighed under 500kg: that's just one-fifth of the weight of a Rolls-Royce Phantom!

HOW TO SPOT ONE

CUTE FACE
Little bug eyes, no great gaping grille… isn't it sweet?

SOFT OR HARD
Fiat 500s came with either a fixed roof or a canvas top that folded back towards the rear window.

MINIATURE
Like the original Mini, the 500 was just three metres long and weighed just 500kg. It looks like a dwarf beside modern cars!

ORIGINAL FIAT 500

15 POINTS

SU 4136 E

OLD BEETLE

One of the only cars in the world hated by Jeremy, James AND Richard. The VW Beetle first turned up in 1938 and was amazingly popular (with everyone apart from *TG* presenters): over 21 MILLION Beetles were sold over the next sixty-five years! Despite its success – and the fact that the original Porsche 911 was based upon it – the Beetle remains *Top Gear's* Public Enemy Number One. Stay vigilant!

ORIGINAL BEETLE

5 POINTS

HOW TO SPOT ONE

ENGINE IN THE BACK
Unlike the modern, front-engined Beetle, the original had its engine in the boot.

BIG FENDERS
Over front and rear wheels.

SILVER WHEELS
The original Beetles' wheels were solid, mirror-like discs.

OLD VW SCIROCCO

Like the new VW Scirocco, the 1974 original was based on a Golf but wrapped up in a much slinkier coupé body. The original Scirocco was killed off in 1992, and remained dead for sixteen years until Volkswagen introduced the modern version in 2008...

ORIGINAL SCIROCCO

10 POINTS

HOW TO SPOT ONE

THREE DOORS
Like the current Scirocco, the old one was a three-door, but with a much curvier 'coupé' backside than the Golf.

FOUR HEADLIGHTS
The Scirocco's wide, straight face is its giveaway feature. The older cars had round headlights, while those built after 1982 had square ones.

BLACK PLASTIC BUMPERS
Forget the colour-coded bumpers of modern cars – most Sciroccos had big, no-nonsense lumps of black plastic to protect against scrapes when parking.

WHEELS

Wheels: all cars have them, but some are weirder than others. Keep your eyes open for these rare sights in the world of tyres!

SPACE-SAVER SPARE

Many modern cars don't have a full-sized spare wheel to replace a punctured tyre. Instead, they make do with a skinny 'space saver' wheel only suitable for travelling a short distance at lower speeds. Fast cars with fat tyres look entirely daft with a space-saver wheel: like a sturdy rhino with one tiny stick-leg!

SPACE-SAVER SPARE

20 POINTS

FLAT TYRE

If you've got a flat tyre, you should stop straight away and change it. But you'd be surprised how many drivers will rumble on for miles without any air in their wheel! If you spot a flat tyre, make sure you do two things. One, let the driver of the car know they're running on the rim... and have some points!

IMPORTANT SCORING NOTE: You can only score points if the car's moving – no points for spotting a flat tyre on a rusty wreck abandoned in a field!

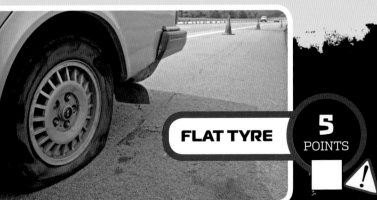

FLAT TYRE

5 POINTS

WHITE-WALL TYRES

20 POINTS

WHITE-WALL TYRES

We'll be impressed if you spy a set of these! Whitewall tyres were mega-popular in the USA in the 1950s, but have gradually been replaced by boring, sensible, all-black rubber. Because they're ultra-cool, they're worth a bag of points if you see a car wearing them. But no cheating with a pot of Tippex! ™

SPINNERS

No, not a slow bowler in cricket, but funny shiny hubcaps that rotate at a different speed to the outside of the wheel. *Top Gear* doesn't really understand spinners, but apparently they're very popular with rap musicians. Often seen on modern music television, have some points if you can spot them out on the road!

SPINNERS

5 POINTS

ROAD KILL

Some grown-ups would probably prefer it if we didn't mention animals getting splattered on the road, but what they don't realise is that roadkill-spotting is a vital part of identifying Britain's wildlife.

Problem is, after an animal's been squished by a car, it becomes a bit tricky to identify what sort of creature it originally was. A stoat looks a lot like a weasel after it's been flattened by a 40-tonne lorry.

DID YOU KNOW?
Inventive cooks have concocted dozens of 'roadkill recipes', including Roast Hedgehog With Nettle Pudding, Badger Fricasee and Moose-And-Squirrel Meatballs! You can even buy 'roadkill cookbooks'. Probably not such a good idea for granny's birthday present...

So we've made it a bit simpler by separating roadkill into three easy-to-identify categories:

5 POINTS

A MAMMAL (FURRY)

10 POINTS

A BIRD (FEATHERY)

100 POINTS

A FISH (SCALY)

We're not quite sure if anyone's ever actually seen fish roadkill before, but if you do, let us know!

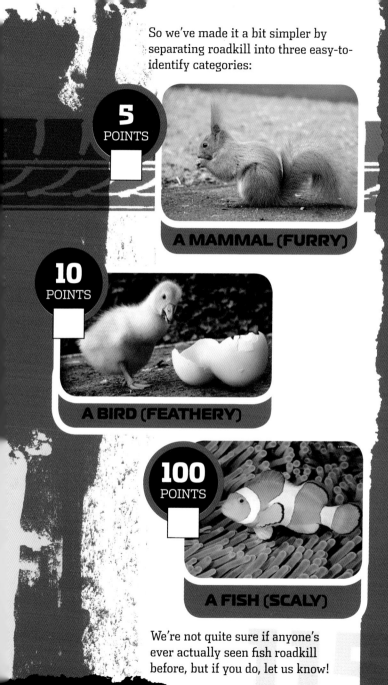

UP IN THE AIR

If there's not much happening down on the road, take a look up in the sky. You never know what you might spot... but please don't try this if you're driving!

HOT AIR BALLOON

Did you know hot air balloons are the oldest form of human air transport? Way back in 1783, a pair of Frenchmen took to the skies, suspended in a basket under a big bag of warm air. Their top speed wasn't recorded, but most historians believe they travelled quicker than James May has ever managed in his Cessna plane!

HOT AIR BALLOON | **5** POINTS

HELICOPTER

People will often tell you that Leonardo da Vinci invented the helicopter, but we don't believe them. We've checked through the helicopter pilot licence records and can't find a Mr Da Vinci anywhere! But guess who DOES have a chopper licence? Richard Hammond. If you spot a pair of very white teeth behind the joystick of a helicopter near you, run for cover!

2 POINTS | **HELICOPTER**

PARACHUTIST

As *Top Gear* proved a few years back, it is possible to parachute into the back of a moving car. However, it's also very dangerous and a bit stupid. If you spot a parachutist floating gently to the ground, please don't try and catch them in your car – they won't appreciate it!

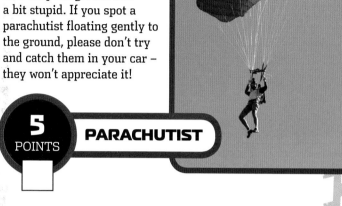

5 POINTS

PARACHUTIST

CARAVAN AIRSHIP

As invented by James May. The caravan airship provides wonderful views for passengers, and removes lumbering caravans from the road, but is almost entirely at the mercy of prevailing winds. If you spot one, it might be worth warning any airports in the local area!

CARAVAN AIRSHIP

50 POINTS

TOWING

F or years, *Top Gear* thought a towball was some sort of very tiny football. Turns out it's actually a hook on the back of your car that hitches to a caravan or trailer, allowing you to merrily tow stuff from one end of the country to the other, causing huge tailbacks as you go. Keep an eye out for these items being dragged behind unwilling cars...

CARAVAN

Top Gear's sworn enemy. Jeremy, James and Richard have spent the last decade destroying these slow, lumbering road menaces in a range of inventive fashions – using them as giant conkers, setting fire to them, turning them into train carriages and THEN setting fire to them – but there are still thousands of caravans left on Britain's roads. Hunt them down, score some points, then give the foolish caravanists your sternest look of disappointment as you overtake.

DON'T CONFUSE IT WITH...

MOTORHOME

While caravans are towed behind cars and can be detached, a motorhome is a sort of caravan built directly around the car. Though they're hardly *Top Gear's* favourite vehicles, they're less offensive than caravans. No points if you spot one of these.

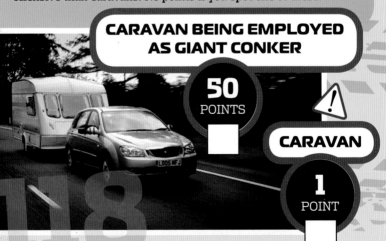

CARAVAN BEING EMPLOYED AS GIANT CONKER

50 POINTS

CARAVAN

1 POINT

118

BOAT

Boats are very good at speeding across water, but not so good on dry land. So if you want to get your marine vessel from one lake to another, and there's no convenient stretch of water linking the two, there's only thing for it: hitch it up to your car!

BOAT

3 POINTS

HORSEBOX

In the olden days, in the era known as 'BC' (we're pretty sure this stands for 'Before Clarkson'), horses were the only form of long-distance transport. Nowadays horses have it easy: if they need to get to the other end of the country, they simply hop into their horsebox and order their owner to drive! Score points for spotting a horsebox... but only if it's got a filly, foal, nag or stallion inside. No horse, no points!

HORSEBOX WITH HORSE

2 POINTS

RACE CAR

Most race cars aren't road-legal: in other words, if you try to drive one on a motorway you'll end up in front of a very angry judge. Shortly after this point, you will end up without a driving licence or any money. That's why you'll see them being towed round the country from race to race on a trailer...

RACE CAR BEING TOWED

3 POINTS

HOUSE

No, we don't mean a caravan – even though that is, technically, a house on wheels. We mean an actual, full-size house. OK, you probably won't see a three-storey mansion being towed down the road, but you might just spot a small bungalow on the back of a VERY big truck. Chances are it'll be flanked by a few policemen making sure everyone else is well out of the way!

HOUSE ON THE MOVE

3 POINTS

ON THE ROOF

If it won't fit in the car and you don't want to tow it, there are only two solutions: leave it behind, or stick it on the roof! Can you spot these (mostly) common items securely tied to the top of cars?

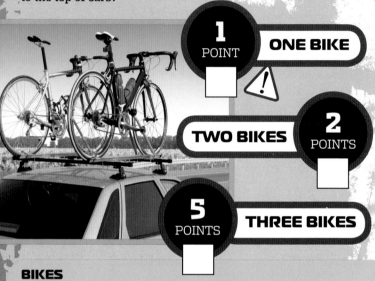

1 POINT — **ONE BIKE** ⚠️

TWO BIKES — **2 POINTS**

5 POINTS — **THREE BIKES**

BIKES

Unless you're a medal-winning Olympic cyclist or you live at the top of a VERY steep hill, it's tough to make a bike go over 50mph. That is, unless you strap it to the roof of a car and head off down the motorway! Now, we're going to have introduce an Important Regulation here: you'll only get points if the bike (or even bikes) are strapped to the ROOF of the car. No points if they're on the back.

CANOES

Top Gear doesn't really understand the difference between a canoe and a kayak, apart from the fact that one is spelled the same forwards as well as backwards, and the other isn't. So have points for spotting canoes, kayaks – in fact, any water-going vessel – strapped to the roof of a car. Even Richard's Dampervan. Or a cruise liner...

ONE CANOE

1 POINT

TWO CANOES

3 POINTS

LADDERS

Ladders: very useful for reaching the top of buildings. Also impossible to transport inside a car, unless you're driving Jeremy's ridiculous Fiat Panda limo. Chances are you'll spot a ladder strapped to the top of a builder's white van, but have extra points if you spy one atop a normal family car...

5 POINTS **LADDER ON CAR**

1 POINT **LADDER ON VAN**

DEAD COW

Clearly only a complete imbecile would attempt to transport a fully-grown, recently deceased bovine on the roof of his car. In fact, we can't think of anyone in the world who would be stupid enough to try such a thing...

DEAD COW ON A CAR

50 POINTS

OPTIONAL EXTRAS

AIR FRESHENER ON REAR-VIEW MIRROR

2 POINTS

PINE TREE SHAPED AIR FRESHENER ON REAR-VIEW MIRROR

Stay Fresh

5 POINTS

NODDING DOG IN A CAR

1 POINT

WINDSCREEN STRIPS

2 POINTS

WINDSCREEN STRIP WITH THE DRIVER'S NAME ON IT

2 POINTS

BABY ON BOARD SIGN

1 POINT

BABY ON BOARD

SO, WHAT DID YOU SCORE?

Whether you're playing alone or against family and friends, you can use these pages to keep track of your scores. Who did you beat and where were you going? And what was the strangest thing you spotted on that trip to granny's house?

JOURNEY	SCORE	OPPONENT

THEIR SCORE	COOLEST SPOT	WEIRDEST SPOT

125